Selections from
Tom Jones Reload

Piano Vocal Guitar

Published 2000
Editor: Anna Joyce

International
MUSIC
Publications

International Music Publications Limited
Griffin House 161 Hammersmith Road London W6 8BS England

MORLINGS LTD.
The House of Music
LOWESTOFT
'Phone (01502) 565491

BURNING DOWN THE HOUSE

Words and Music by David Byrne,
Chris Frantz, Tina Weymouth and Jerry Harrison

MAMA TOLD ME NOT TO COME

Words and Music by Randy Newman

me not to come. Ma-ma said_ that ain't the way to have fun._

ARE YOU GONNA GO MY WAY

Words and Music by
Lenny Kravitz and Craig Ross

14

VERSE 2:
I don't know why we always cry,
This we must leave and get undone.
We must engage and rearrange
And turn this planet back to one.
So tell me why we got to die
And kill each other one by one.
We've got to hug and rub-a-dub,
We've got to dance and be in love.
But what I really want to know is
Are you gonna go my way?
And I got to, got to know.

SUNNY AFTERNOON

Words and Music by Ray Davies

I'M LEFT, YOU'RE RIGHT, SHE'S GONE

Words and Music by
Stanley A. Kesler and William E. Taylor

SEXBOMB

Words and Music by
Mousse T. and Errol Rennalls

YOU NEED LOVE LIKE I DO
(DON'T YOU)

Words and Music by
Norman Whitfield and Barrett Strong

LUST FOR LIFE

Words and Music by
David Bowie and James Osterberg

lo - tion.   I   been   hurt-in' since I   bought   the gim - mick a-bout
priz - es   I'm through sleep-in' on the   side - walk, no   more
(𝄋) Your skin starts it - chin' once you   buy   the gim - mick a-bout

some-thing called   love,   (𝄋) yeah,   some-thing called love.   Well,
beat - in' my   brains,   no more beat - in'   my   brains   with
some-thing called   love,

that's   like   hyp - no - tiz - ing   chick-ens.
liq-uor and drugs,   with   liq-uor and drugs.

Well, I'm just _ a mod-ern guy. _   Of course I've had it in _ the

LOOKING OUT MY WINDOW

Words and Music by Tom Jones

LITTLE GREEN BAG

Words and Music by
Hans Bouwens and Jan Visser

SHE DRIVES ME CRAZY

Words and Music by
David Steele and Roland Gift

1. I can't help   the way I feel,—
2. I can't get   a - ny rest,—

things you   do—   don't seem   so— real.—   Mmm.
peo - ple   say—   I'm   ob - sessed.—

59

(AIN'T THAT) A LOT OF LOVE

Words and Music by
Willia Dean Parker and Homer Banks

NEVER TEAR US APART

Words and Music by
Andrew Farriss and Michael Hutchence

66

67

BABY, IT'S COLD OUTSIDE

Words and Music by Frank Loesser

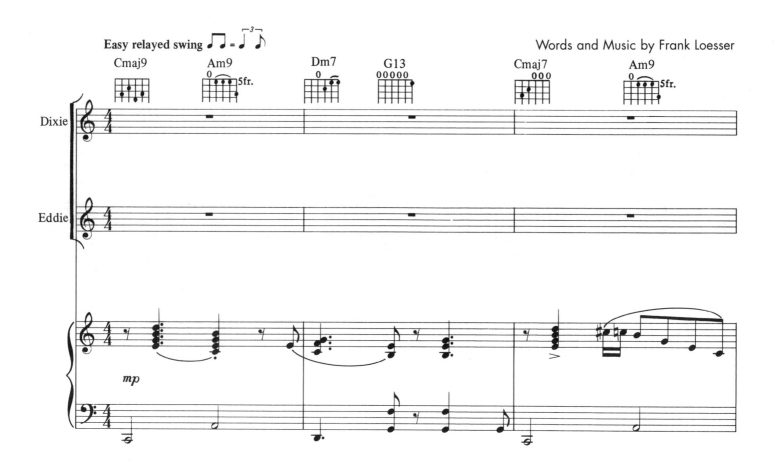

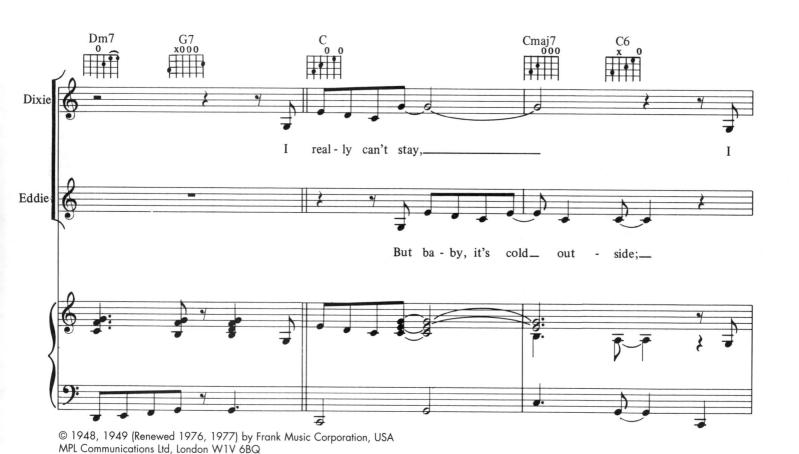

Dixie: I real-ly can't stay,_____ I

Eddie: But ba-by, it's cold___ out-side;___

MOTHERLESS CHILD

Traditional

Have You Tried These Other Great Music Books From International Music Publications?

Celine Dion
6743A   PVG

Includes: All By Myself – Because You Loved Me – Falling Into You – Immortality – Just A Little Bit Of Love – Love Can Move Mountains – My Heart Will Go On (Love Theme from "Titanic") – Only One Road – The Power Of Love – The Reason – Tell Him – Think Twice

Tom Jones
6744A   PVG

Includes: Burning Down The House – Daughter Of Darkness – Delilah – Green Green Grass Of Home – I'll Never Fall In Love Again – I'm Coming Home – It's Not Unusual – Kiss – Sexbomb – Thunderball – Till – What's New Pussycat – With These Hands – You Can Leave Your Hat On

Cher
6747A   PVG

Includes: Believe – Gypsies, Tramps And Thieves – I Found Someone – I Got You Babe – If I Could Turn Back Time – Just Like Jesse James – The Shoop Shoop Song (It's In His Kiss) – Strong Enough – Walking In Memphis

Madonna
6746A   PVG

Includes: Beautiful Stranger – Crazy For You – Frozen – Holiday – Like A Prayer – Like A Virgin – Material Girl – Papa Don't Preach – Ray Of Light – This Used To Be My Playground – Who's That Girl?

Whitney Houston
7187A   PVG

Includes: The Greatest Love Of All – How Will I Know – I Wanna Dance With Somebody (Who Loves Me) – I Will Always Love You – I'm Every Woman – It's Not Right But It's Okay – Love Will Save The Day – My Love Is Your Love – One Moment In Time – Saving All My Love For You

Sheryl Crow
7391A   Guitar Tab / Vocal

Includes: All I Wanna Do – Anything But Down – Can't Cry Anymore – Everyday Is A Winding Road – If It Makes You Happy – Leaving Las Vegas – My Favourite Mistake – Run Baby Run – Strong Enough – There Goes The Neighbourhood

Gary Moore
6745A   Guitar Tab / Vocal

Includes: Cold Day In Hell – Empty Rooms – One Fine Day – Out In The Fields – Over The Hills And Far Away – Parisienne Walkways – Separate Ways – Still Got The Blues – Story Of The Blues – What Are We Here For?

Flying Without Wings
& 9 More Great Chart Hits
6743A   PVG

Includes: As Time Goes By – (Ain't That) A Lot Of Love – Flying Without Wings – I Try – Millennium Prayer – New York City Boy – S Club Party – Summertime Of Our Lives – Sunshine – When We Are Together – Unpretty

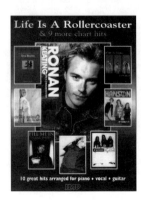

LIFE IS A ROLLERCOASTER
& 9 MORE CHART HITS
7490A   PVG

Includes: Dancing In The Moonlight – Dirty Water – Fill Me In – Genie In A Bottle – Life Is A Rollercoaster – If Only – Life Story – Sex Bomb – Sitting Down Here – So Long

ABC
& 9 More Funky Disco Hits
7207A   PVG

Includes: ABC – Ain't No Stopping Us Now – Boogie Wonderland – Dancing Queen – I'm So Excited – Lost In Music – Move On Up – We Are Family – Y.M.C.A. – You Make Me Feel Like Dancing

International Music Publications Ltd
Griffin House 161 Hammersmith Road London England W6 8BS

International MUSIC Publications

GH2

7601A

7602A

7603A